The Ramblings of a Madman

A.T Hittles

BookLeaf
Publishing

India | USA | UK

Presentation by *BookLeaf Publishing*

Web: www.bookleafpub.com

E-mail: info@bookleafpub.com

ISBN: 9789357449137

First edition 2022

DEDICATION

To Patricia, who always taught me the value of reading.

To Stacey, thank you. Sempre Simile.

ACKNOWLEDGEMENT

I'd like to give a special shout out to Sam;

I cast you out bud.
Rest now, shuffle towards the dying of the light.
I've got this from here.

PREFACE

I would like to let everybody know that it's
going to be okay.

Your struggles are valid and will always be hard
but I know that you can get through this.

You have worth;
The only thing this world cannot take from you
is your smile.

And as the Devil Spoke

Hello again, How are you there?
Surely you must be well?
Knowing that you've fallen down and ended up
in hell.

No chance of saviour nor of safety, in the bowels
of hell. We have lots of tea and hearty chats
there's lots to do as well.

Please do not be scared and do not fret.
We are all delightfully mad.
That's what happens when you spend and
eternity being bad.

What happens now?
You may ask.
When you face the burn
You've come down here simply because my dear
it is your turn.

So come on down let's not delay.
You've got some thinking do
Just think about what you have done.
You rotten fucker, You.

And as the Devil Spoke, I did.

An Agnostics Prayer

For a moment I questioned God and my
thoughts returned to me.

"Who are you to question me? A speck of my
eternity, a moment of all originality, a fraction of
who you are, to be."

So, my thoughts they stilled, quietly.

Time/Entropy

The Dual Sided God.
Time is healing and patience.
Entropy is decay and inevitably inevitable.

Both are one, it all truly depends on what frame
of mind you are in.
Time is kind, Entropy malicious, the coin, the
con and the constant reminder, Of what was and
what is to come.

Time and Entropy are great friends with Karma.

As neither are truly evil or good.
Just undeniable constants.

Karma

The most powerful and most kind.
The most passive and corrupt.
Karma is a force, one who can only believe in
you if you believe in her.

She believes that what you give is what you get.

She believe that being 'bad' is absolutely
destructive, then you allow her to rule you for
your actions.
By your own faults.

Live kind, you will never have to worry about
her.

Those who don't, will.

Hope

5

I believe in Hope

I believe that wishes and wants are paramount to
success, those able to drive themselves to always
be better, be faster, be kinder, be more today
than last; should always find a hope.

A belief that it will all work out, provided they
never ever stop to doubt themselves or sit on
their collective hands and let 'fate' sort it all out.

Fate

I've never been one to believe in fate. Such a strange word for those eager to string a bunch of coincidences together to tell those daring that they mean something to the universe. Those who believe that they are bound to some predetermined timeline, to faith or to some divine entity; could allow themselves hope in some unshakeable plan that they know not of.

Destiny is more appropriate I believe, and nearly everyone is in charge of that at least.

Memories (most manly menacing)

Remember, all of it now, does no good to lie;
stand up straight, where's that smile? Go on,
show your soul minus thought for a while.
Reflection through self and sanity, retain
nevertire, most degrading of course for a liar.

Mostly my memory makes no sense to me.
Mumbled, jumbled and many degrading
maliciously. My masters mock me but never
seem to stop me, making my markings an item
for the mockery, my ego not as shallow as my
heart always seems to beat. Many mark me
thicker, I'm just quicker. Most make me mainly
mind my manners reminding me of the clangers,
in the marked molasses of my mind's
manhandling and rambling.

Yet, the best thing about the past is that it's
history. Best forgiving and forgotten, then you
get your bliss for free. Remind your mind to
rewind for a symphony; before becoming
unbecoming is normality, before everyone sees
you, the you that you'd never be.

So put on that show.

Let them all see.

The Loneliness of Me.

I don't like people.

I also do not like being alone.

I honestly wonder some days if I'm strong
enough.

I honestly wonder which is stronger;
The me, with the desire to be the best version of
myself or the next who can be sociable, the
scallywag, the fool in most other's eyes.

Weirdly enough I'm at ease when I have a drink
in my hand, it also has to be alcoholic.

So I can forget the me that remembers, ignore
the me that is me and forgive my past, if only for
a moment.

The Red View

Anger is truly my fatal flaw, all have one. That one flaw that will be the death of themselves.

Yeah.

Mine is an unshakeable, undeniable rage that stubbornly stabs at my soul and shakes the system, nay even the damn world to its core; screaming.

The red haze of it all, my past, all my hate; and least if all my suffering I'd my crutch.

I try now to view it as a motivator. I hold my anger, tight and I never let the fuck go. Never give in to see that view of complete destruction, but I can't quite seem to shake it, because even when I turn it off, It still won't go away.

The Insomniac's Prayer

-and in this passive morn, I lay awake.
Wanting now some kind of break.
Perhaps I should drift away,
Thou it holds me steady at its bay.
 For once again I lay awake
For there is no rest to take.

Reflections

I see a new thing.
Not sure what.
Not sure how.
But he's there.

I look at his face.
Red, glowing eyes.
Sharp, gnawing teeth.
Scars,too numerous.

I double take.
I touch his face.
Feel the rough edges.
And gasped.

I see a new thing
This time i'm sure.
The thing i see.
In a mirror.

I stopped believing in Monsters....
The day I became one.
And I do not, not I, suffer from Insanity.
I enjoy every moment.

A cliff.

A man is on the edge of a cliff. This man he has nothing except for the clothes on his back. He has no memories, no thought, no hope. He stands on the edge of the cliff. At the bottom of the cliff is darkness. A churning unrelenting sea of chaos; the embodiment of Nyx.

The man hears a voice.

"Jump."

The voice itself was peaceful. Seemingly kind and gentle.

The man, having no memories, no thought and no hope, jumps.

There is no happy ending here.
Just darkness.
Everlasting Darkness.

Pity; near the end of a broken bottle.

I just don't know where I am going. I need a
helping hand, one to guide me along. One that
makes me need to feel brave, even in when
alone in the dark. I need that signal or sign to
force me along the road less traveled, with
someone with me to make me feel safe.

And so it all winds down, the night of blind
references moving towards blind memories not
knowing when or how or where I'll wake up.
Not knowing why I chose this or that. Not caring
for either. Chances taken or lost. Alcohol: The
haze over a indifferent night.

3:57 am

Some nights I see the world, spinning and slowing. Tearing itself asunder with hurt, pain and flowing - Anger which I know, sometimes corrupts my own soul.

I see the sadness and the empty promises, of men and mice working their way towards greatness and failure - the failure, I am too familiar with.

Some nights I wish that i cannot see the future or the past. Or perhaps, anything at all.

Even the best, fall.

Two sides of the same coin.

It all ends tonight,
The little hopes and dreams.
The daunting repetitive tasks.
That mindless nine to five grind.

It is silence,
The panic in problems.
The fear in the dark.
That meddlesome creature of the night.

It is pain,
The whispers in your head.
The unspoken words of trust.
That interfering brain.

Something holds me.
It's touch noticeable enough.
Making me feel hesitant.
To give myself over to you.

It whispers tiny things.
Things of secrets.

Things of plots.
Against me and all I love.

It wants me to fail.
It wants me to run.
It wants me to jump.
It will never beat me.

Get out / Don't go

Sometimes I have to stop and think about what I am thinking; as if the abrupt craziness of humdrum daydream was enough to stir such a reaction to my own mind. I hear a voice in my head that isn't mine, one that is sardonic and confusing but just wants to talk and has time to, at all times.

I get caught up in a conversation with myself that ends with laughter; as if I prefer the voice that assures me that everything is okay and i have nothing to worry about. No fears with no worries.

I hear whispers that don't belong in my mind, secret things that i may have suspected of myself but still wish i didn't know, or was ignorant enough to ignore. I have my quiet moments sure, everyone does but mine are interrupted by.. well.. me.

It wont stop talking, and i want it and i don't want it to. It depends on the day and my mood.

Which fluctuates at alarming levels nowadays. It just wont be quiet.

Get out of my head.

Don't get out of my head.

The Wolves

See now I remember a time where there were wolves at my door. They bit and fought until they withdrew, mistaking me for dead. I remember that time, the time where I picked myself up, licked my wounds and walked away.

I knew why they were at my door. I left it open for any one to enter destroying my life as they did. I barricaded myself in and never left the safety of the shelter I created.

I made myself into what i am now. Distant, cold and somewhat sardonic in a way to remove my very being from the overall stupidity that is ordinary people.

Dont misunderstand me. People are great although there are some that just shouldnt speak or move or act.

So on the day I opened my door again the wolves were waiting but I made them full of fear; the same that they gave me. I turned them into worse disrepair than I was. They, however, were not strong enough to be well.. strong.

So if I give you the cold shoulder, I apologise to
you now, as I cannot help my nature.

In a moment of weakness, the wolves could
return. And im not letting my guard down.

Not for a minute.

Not for a second.

Not for anyone.

Not anymore.

Aut pati, aut mori. Dilectio sanabat omnes.

Either to suffer or to die. Love healed all.

We were young, dumb and among most other things a bit broken. We used our broken parts to heal one another and got angry when the pieces couldn't fit right.

We smashed and crashed our way through everything, with a 'this is how it is' kind of fashion. Among most other failings. We tried.

We gave our best and my god I wish I could give more. It's so hard being trapped in a self depressive pit of loneliness and regret, but it's a bit harder sharing pits.

We called time out, we rushed in deep and we found ourselves expecting. No one could ever quite believe what they were directing.

We were bliss among all duress, upon us came
stress and then oh no, less and the less and then
more and then oh no everything just hurts.

We were unsure on the feeling of pure
unrelenting endured, anger flash and then more,
words spoken, regrets, never more because
hurting in anyway is what we never wanted so.

Why do we hurt? We poke and we prod, we
attack and we nod, not listening odd, it's funny
because I'm not exactly having fun see, Im just
stressed because what I want is sadly history.

And I miss them and us
And it hurts to be.
Existing isn't bliss anymore for me

I want so badly, and I'm lost.
I need.

Needing

Wishing for the wanting of needing of pleasing
and leaving a trace of something real. Wanting
for the wishing of the pleasing and the needing
whilst drinking from the hell that is life.
But don't drink too much for you will drink
away your soul, but don't die of thirst for you
will die needing.

Wishing for the night to understand your
sadness, so that the day might brighten you.
Wanting to give the night a chance, so that the
day mightn't spite you
Needing the night to give a damn, so that the day
will wake you.
Notting the night to shake you, so the day will
rise again

A hopeful dream

I once had a dream. It was remarkably bright and the future was too. I had a family, kids, house of my own. I had happiness.

Now the dream is scattered and unrealistic; abrasive yet unattainable, as if the stars so willingly aligned themselves in such a fashion that I could only realise the futility of my actions.

The dream; broken in a sea of lies, a bed of borrowed trust, gone to the wish of what was.

My feeling too, odd to say the least, wantonly disloyal to the heart as it wanted loyalty, love and hope.

I hope someday to have that again.

Doubt however;

Evermore.

Supersam

The can do man, the amazing, the dad, the worker, the hoper, the dreamer; the me I wish I was, the scooter man, the driver, the rider, the brother, the father the pushes himself further man.

The kind, the courageous, the guy. At nights, oh the times that I could fly. All around me dropped and died but still I flies, and high did I, except then I didn't.

I fell.

Into a deep depression, unworthy of expression, unrelenting in repression, underlying stress and the tension; of losing life's, based in my ventures.

The fool, the unmanliest man. The Sam.